Where are you going? the phone! You can't take my car. Pick up your clothes. Turn that music down! When will you be home? Do you know what time it is? Take out the trash. Are you wearing that? I don't like your attitude! Where are you? What did you do to your hair? Get out of the shower! Listen! Where are you going?

TEENAGE Expectations

THE REAL PARENT'S GUIDE TO THE TERRIBLE TEENS

Terry Lee Bilsky

Illustrated by Jill Weber

Andrews McMeel
Publishing

Kansas City

Attention: Schools and Businesses

Acknowledgments

Teenage Expectations could not have been written without the help of our friends who have successfully raised teenagers. Since Jill and I remember being perfect teenagers, we have no stories to tell. Therefore, we would like to thank Adelin Bakke, Jeanne Betancourt, Coach Larry Byrnes, Mary Engelbreit, Janet Gardner, Judy and Paul Hartnett, Miki Jaeger, Barbara Price, Barbara Schwartz (Jill's mother who never said I told you so), and JoAnne and Vincent Vicidomini.

We would also like to thank our agent, Janis Donnaud, and our editor, Chris Schillig, for making sure we always do our homework.

For Lee George Bilsky, my future teenager, just remember I wrote the book.— **TLB**

For Remy Martin Weber, not only did we survive your teen years but the outcome is wonderful.— **JW**

For Paul Bilsky and Frank Weber, with our love and gratitude for being such good dads.

Hello! Can you hear me? You can't hear me? The **what** is too loud? Turn down the mu...? **The music !!!!!** Oh, of course, I don't even hear it anymore.... Let me get into that bedroom and shut it off. If I just climb over this pile of clothes and, what are these, wet towels? Where is that boom box? It's getting louder so I must be getting warmer. **Silence!** Ahh, yes, now can you hear me?

Just mention the word teenager and the most loving, caring parents, the ones who had all the answers up to age twelve, break into a cold sweat. Eyebrows are raised, hair stands on end, and arms go up in despair. Not since the "terrible twos" has there been such a universal longing for a stage of development to be over. However, this one runs longer and its challenges are far greater. And you can no longer pick them up, change their clothes, or put them to bed early when you've had enough.

EXPECT

Teenagers to sleep incessantly,
reclaiming their long-abandoned nap.

Mornings to begin at noon.

If they are up before noon, it's because
they haven't gone to bed yet.

EXPECT

Them to think your car is really theirs
(along with everything else).

Never again to find the gas tank full.

To consider yourself lucky
if you have enough fumes left
to get to the nearest gas station.

EXPECT

Closed doors.

Secrets that do not include you.

The same little person who loved to tell you everything
is now a big person who tells you nothing.

EXPECT

Eye rolls.

Deep sighs.

Mood swings.

11

EXPECT

Them to need lots of verbal hugs,
despite their unwillingness to listen.

Teenagers to want your approval
but never ask for it.

Them to do what you suggested
but never while you're looking.

EXPECT

Not to trust a teenager.

An overnight trip to be a thing of the past
while they are too old for a babysitter
and too young to be left alone.

To want to know (do you really?)
but never know where they are at all times.

EXPECT

That as much as they fuss
over how they look when they go out,
what they leave behind is a nightmare.

Their room to smell
like a gymnasium,
whether or not they are in it.

To decide that you like, even prefer,
when they keep their doors closed.

EXPECT

To ask: **"ARE YOU GOING LIKE THAT?????"**

"DO YOU KNOW WHAT TIME IT IS??????"

"WHERE ARE YOU??????"

Your mother to remind you that she asked **you** the same questions.

EXPECT

Phone bills. **Big** phone bills.
Really big phone bills.

To realize that "call waiting"
was invented for teenagers.

The phone to rarely ring for you,
and if it does, not to receive any messages.

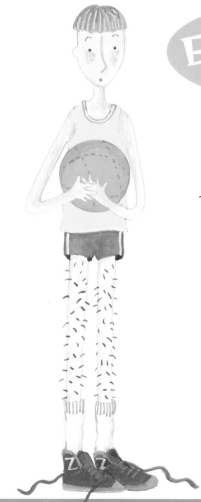

EXPECT

Growth spurts.
Hairy legs and
hormonal changes.
Smelly sneakers
and fragile egos.

EXPECT

Not to understand the meaning of mortality until you have a teenager.

To realize they don't have any idea what mortality is.

DANGER!

BE CAREFUL ♥ SLOW DOWN!

Warning!

EXPECT

Your daughter to have a different shampoo
and conditioner for each day of the week and
a different brand of tampon for every day of the month.

Your son to try a variety of mousse, gel,
shaving cream, and aftershave, but to like
yours the most and to forget to replace it.

EXPECT

NOISE.

To walk in the door and find the television on
and the music blaring but no one home.

To admit you hate their music
even if saying so makes you feel old.

EXPECT

 Them to be more resilient than you are.

That while you redo and rethink,
they move on and bounce back.

To address their heartbreak over yesterday's boyfriend,
unaware they have a new one today.

EXPECT

Your child to become a divisive element
in your marriage, a master
at playing one against the other.

Them to find fault with all the things
about you that they used to love.

Not to be allowed
to sing to them,
kiss them,
or even talk
to them in public.

EXPECT

Grunts at the dinner table.

Never again to be spoken to in complete sentences.

Their response to be either **"cool"** or **"whatever."**

EXPECT

To wish their tattoos would wash off
like they used to when they were toddlers.

Hair to become a statement.

Them to be pierced in places
you don't want to know about.

MOM

EXPECT

To hear that all the other parents said it was okay.

Teenagers to believe that you are clueless and that they will **never** get caught.

Them to want to get caught so they know someone else is in charge.

EXPECT

To feel stupid and to be told,
"you don't understand."

Them to make fun of your clothes,
your hair, your music,
and your social life,
if you still have one.

HA HA HA HA HA

what?

SOUNDS OF the 60's

EXPECT

To discover that some parents really are clueless
and prefer not to know where their kids are
or what they are doing.

To hold your breath whenever your teenager
is invited to certain homes.

Never to see your child alone again.

Their friends to be all that matter to them.

Them not to agree to a family vacation
or an outing of any kind
unless friends are invited.

EXPECT

To get to know the police on a first-name basis.

That if you ground them, you'll find yourself grounded too.

To have the following conversation late at night:
"Our house? They're not at our house! I thought they were at your house! WHERE ARE THEY???"

29

EXPECT

To regret the day you ever criticized anyone else's kid.

To enjoy the time away
from your teenager more
than the time with your teenager.

Other people to like your kids
more than you do.

EXPECT

It to be easier to move a mountain than convince a teenager to do a simple chore.

To be tempted to do it yourself.

To find yourself in mortal combat over washing the dishes or walking the dog.

EXPECT

Scary dreams, as in
"I left my teenager home alone."

That "having a couple of friends over"
could amount to a couple of hundred.

If they confess to having had eight girls over,
you can be sure there were that many boys.

EXPECT

To become a human **ATM**.

To share your credit card for "emergency use only."

When your bill arrives, to wonder what emergencies might have occurred at Tower Records.

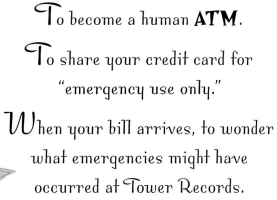

EXPECT

Tall tales.
Hushed tones.
Whispered conversations.

EXPECT

To wish they would simply sit down
and do their homework like they used to,
instead of waiting until midnight to begin.

To hate final exams and
feel familiar rumblings in your lower stomach.

MATH

EXPECT

Sex to be the first thing on their mind.

To never want them having it under your roof.

To find yourself in a drugstore (not in your neighborhood), discreetly buying condoms, and to discover they make great stocking stuffers.

EXPECT

To feel a pang of envy as you become aware
that along with having youth on their side,
they have no ties, no responsibilities, and
no one to answer to (except for you,
and they don't listen to you anyhow).

EXPECT

The return of sleep deprivation while you:

Answer the phone at 3 A.M.

Wait to hear a key in the door.

Find yourself searching for bodies in their beds.

EXPECT

Clothes and hair that make it hard to recognize them.

Them to never want to recognize you.

To find yourself the invisible and ignored chauffeur until the dreaded words: "Can I have the car keys?"

EXPECT

That if there is one box of cereal,
they will eat one box.

That if there are eight boxes,
they will eat all eight.

There never to be enough food in the house.

Pants that are too big and skirts that are too short.

Broken hearts and broken-out skin.

Them to need hugs even if they no longer fit on your lap.

To like hear the word **"like"** more than,
like, you ever did before, and, **like,** to notice that,
like, most sentences end with, **like,** a question mark
even though they are not, **like,** really questions???

Like, **WHATever...**

EXPECT

*Y*our teenagers to dress, talk, and look the same as their friends.

*T*hem not to want to stand out or dare to be different.

*T*hat if they do decide to wear something different, it will be an impossible item, not found in any store on this earth and it will be all your fault.

43

EXPECT

Wet towels.

To run out of hot water after their never-ending third shower of the day.

To hide your razor if you ever want another clean shave.

EXPECT

The same teenager who is absolutely awful,
disgusting, and horrible in November
to turn into a terrific person in February.

To wish grown-ups were capable
of this kind of change.

EXPECT

To miss being able to cuddle, but learn to be grateful for a lanky arm over your shoulder, a leg across your lap, or an occasional peck on your cheek.

To think better of them than they think of themselves.

EXPECT

That just as things begin to get better,
it's time for them to go away to college.

To hope they're ready.

To know that an entire stage of their life and yours has passed.

To cry for the first week (or month, or semester).

To miss their friends, the food shopping, the wet towels,
the phone calls, the smelly bedroom, and, okay, even the music.

To suddenly see the promise and excitement
of sending them into this world.

To try to remember what **was** so bad about having a teenager.

Whatever. You don't understand It's not my fault! What do you mean I can't go? Everyone else is going! What's the matter with my hair? All the other parents said "yes." Like, whatever. Get off my back! Sorry. In a minute! There isn't anything good to eat. I'll do it later! Like I even care. I didn't know what time it was. I'll pay you back later. Whatever!